Willie Dixon's Blues

A Talk with Marie Dixon

by Robert Jackson

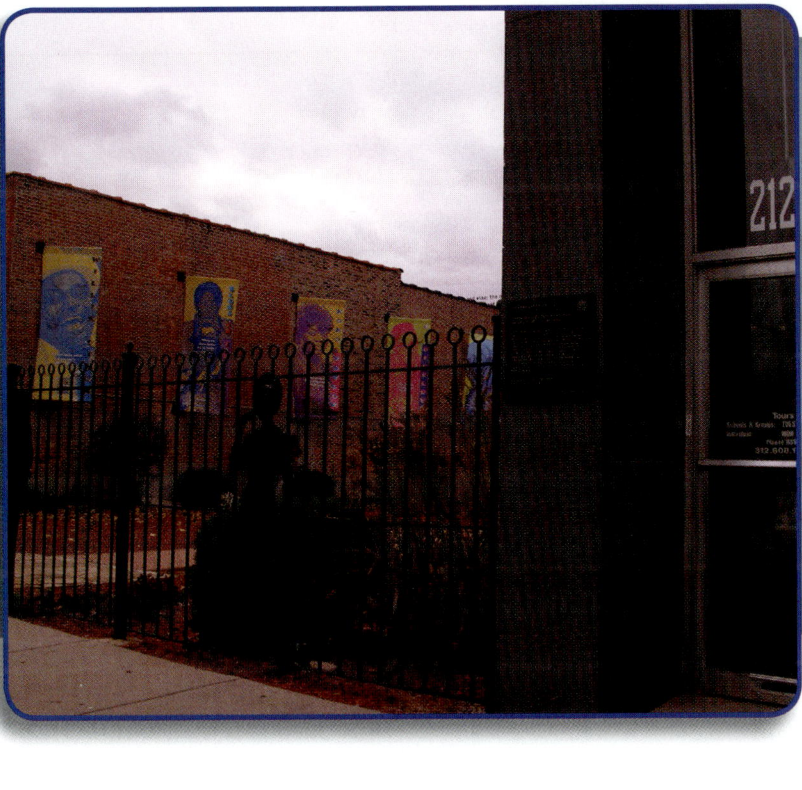

PEARSON
Scott Foresman

Editorial Offices: Glenview, Illinois • Parsippany, New Jersey • New York, New York
Sales Offices: Needham, Massachusetts • Duluth, Georgia • Glenview, Illinois
Coppell, Texas • Sacramento, California • Mesa, Arizona

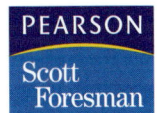

Willie Dixon (1915–1992)

Willie Dixon devoted his whole life to blues music. Willie sang the blues, played the blues, and wrote more than 500 blues songs.

Willie once said, "The blues are the roots, and the other musics are the fruits." Willie was saying that other types of American music—such as jazz, gospel, and rock and roll—could not exist if the blues had not come first. Blues music is both sad and lively.

After a wonderful career, Willie Dixon died in 1992. Since then, his wife Marie Dixon has continued helping blues musicians, just as Willie had done.

In 2004, I had the chance to talk to Ms. Dixon about her husband, about blues music, and about her life. Here are my favorite parts of my interview, or conversation, with Marie Dixon.

Interview with Marie Dixon

What are "the blues"? The answer depends on whom you ask. Some people talk about a type of music. Others talk about sadness and worry in life. I asked Marie Dixon what the blues meant to her.

"As Willie said, the blues are the true facts of life, expressed in words and song, inspiration, feeling, and understanding."

I asked her to explain. "The blues express people's feelings," she said. "It's just about life."

My next question was, "Where did the blues come from?"

"I don't know if there's a certain place," she began. "They [the blues] came from life, from the world." Later, she explained that she meant life in the world of slavery, everywhere people were enslaved.

Marie Dixon

---

inspiration: something that has a strong effect on what you feel or do, especially something good

Marie Dixon shares a happy memory about her husband Willie.

Then I asked Ms. Dixon to tell me about herself.

"I was born in Oxford, Mississippi," she began. "I came to Chicago when I was sixteen years old."

Coming to Chicago was a big change, but "life was fun," she said. Then she started telling me how she met Willie.

She had gone with some friends to a club ". . . to see a different performer."

I asked, "Were you attracted to the music or the man?"

"It was the music," she began. Then she politely let me know that it was Willie who had been attracted to Marie. "But nothing came of it at the time," she said.

She continued:

> About two years later I was working at a drug store . . . and he came in there and reintroduced himself. From that day forward we became friends, we became husband and wife, and we had five children.

---

club: restaurant that offers entertainment such as music

Willie in a recording studio with his bass

Willie Dixon had many talents. He was a singer, a songwriter, a bass player, and an arranger. I asked Marie if she would like to add anything to that list. She did. "He was a perfect father and husband—a wonderful man."

It was easy to see that Marie loved her husband very much. She continued:

> You could not meet anyone greater than Willie Dixon. He was a man of joy, and a man of a lot of pain. But he could take his pain and still find happiness in it.

---

bass: a bass fiddle; a large stringed musical instrument that makes a low, deep sound

arranger: someone who decides what each musician should play and what each voice should sing for a piece of music

I asked Marie to tell me how Chicago became a center for the blues. She said:

People in the South heard about going up North. Some had played music in the South . . . Willie had been with a gospel group.

She told me that blues musicians began to hear stories:

. . . they could come to Chicago and get an audience to listen instead of having two or three people sitting in one room listening to their music. And this is how Chicago became the center of urban blues . . . (the musicians) migrated from all over the South to Chicago.

Many blues musicians came to Chicago in the 1930s.

urban: big city
migrated: moved from one place to settle in another

Memphis Slim, born John Chapman, played the piano.

For blues musicians, it was easier to make money in Chicago. But they had other problems. As African Americans, they were treated unfairly, during that time in United States history. Marie told me what Willie and Memphis Slim decided to do about this. She said:

> In about 1960 Willie went to Paris, France. He felt that he had something to offer, and he was not getting the respect he wanted in the United States.

Marie explained that going to Paris was a hard thing to do. But they went. "Willie said, 'You know, I'm going to take my music somewhere else, because nobody is listening to me.'"

The trip was a success. Many people in Europe did appreciate American blues. Willie helped to bring many blues musicians to Europe in 1962.

As a young woman, Marie Dixon heard Mahalia Jackson (left) sing at her local church.

I then asked Marie about gospel music. Did she see a connection between gospel music and blues?

"There is a connection . . . sometimes it's in suffering, pain, and disappointment."

Marie told me about the great gospel singer Mahalia Jackson. "She used to attend a church that I also attended here in Chicago. She would be there and perform on various Sundays."

Marie said she loved to listen to Mahalia sing. "She had such a great voice . . . She was very inspirational to me, and still is. As a matter of fact, I have a tape of hers out in my car right now."

---

gospel music: a kind of music that began in African American churches

suffering: pain or great sadness

disappointment: the feeling you have when you do not get what you expected or hoped for

But as much as Marie loved gospel music, she was "married to the blues." I asked her to talk about some other blues singers, besides her husband Willie.

I asked her first about Koko Taylor. "I know Koko very well," Marie said with pride. "Koko is a great performer. Willie was the first to discover Koko...."

Willie also wrote a song for Koko that was a big hit. But Koko's career, or life as a singer, was not always easy for her.

"She has paid great dues in this world to get to be called the Queen of the Blues," Marie told me.

I asked Marie how Koko was doing these days.

"We just celebrated her birthday over at Buddy Guy's club," she said. "And she is still performing!" (Buddy Guy is a blues musician.)

Koko Taylor is a blues singer and was a friend of Willie Dixon.

---

paid great dues: lived through many bad things

Willie Dixon's granddaughter, Keshia Dixon Nelson

While we were talking, Marie mentioned her granddaughter, Keshia. She wanted me to meet Keshia before I left.

"She's downstairs. I'll get her up here," Marie said. "She's writing songs now. She's got about ten songs she's written."

While we waited for Keshia to come upstairs, Marie told me a few things about her. "Willie taught her to blow blues harmonica in her high chair," she laughed.

Then, more seriously, she talked about Willie Dixon's funeral. Keshia was three years old at the time. With her brother, Keshia sang one of Willie's favorite songs. The song is called "It Don't Make Sense If You Can't Make Peace."

Finally, Keshia joined us. She told me that she knows how lucky she is as a young singer to have family friends like Koko Taylor. Keshia told me that she had already performed a few times. She sang in the Blues Heaven Garden during the past summer.

Willie Dixon had begun the Blues Heaven Foundation, a group that helps elderly blues performers and teaches children about the blues.

The Blues Heaven Garden in Chicago

I asked Keshia to sing something for us. She sang a song that she wrote called "Blues Woman."

Keshia sang beautifully. Some day, she might be a famous blues singer.

As I was leaving, Marie Dixon had some final thoughts about Willie. "He was an easy man to know," she said.

Even after Willie became famous, he still treated everyone the same.

"He didn't care where you came from. He would say, 'Sit down to the table and let's have some food.'"

And this kind woman, Marie Dixon, clearly felt the same way.

"It was a delight to talk to you," I said. It truly was a delight.